The More Extravagant Feast

Winner of the Walt Whitman Award
of the Academy of American Poets
2019
Selected by Li-Young Lee

Sponsored by the Academy of American Poets,
the Walt Whitman Award is given annually to the winner
of an open competition among American poets
who have not yet published a book of poems.

The More Extravagant Feast

poems

Leah Naomi Green

Graywolf Press

This publication is made possible, in part, by the voters of Minnesota through a Minnesota State Arts Board Operating Support grant, thanks to a legislative appropriation from the arts and cultural heritage fund. Significant support has also been provided by the McKnight Foundation, Target, the Lannan Foundation, the Amazon Literary Partnership, and other generous contributions from foundations, corporations, and individuals. To these organizations and individuals we offer our heartfelt thanks.

Published by Graywolf Press
250 Third Avenue North, Suite 600
Minneapolis, Minnesota 55401

www.graywolfpress.org

Published in the United States of America

ISBN 978-1-64445-018-5

2 4 6 8 9 7 5 3 1
First Graywolf Printing, 2020

Library of Congress Control Number: 2019933486

Cover design: Jeenee Lee Design

Cover photo: Sally Mann © 1999

For Ben, June, and Robin on her way

My tongue, every atom of my blood, form'd from this soil, this air,
Born here of parents born here from parents the same, and their parents the same.
—Walt Whitman

Contents

IV. *The More Extravagant Feast*

The More Extravagant Feast

I

Seed and Fugue

Field Guide to the Chaparral

The fire beetle only mates
when the chaparral is burning

and the water beetle
will only mate in the rain.

In the monastery kitchen, the nuns
don't believe me

when I tell them how old I am,
that you were married before.

The woman you find attractive
does not believe me when I look at her kindly.

There are candescent people in the world.
It will only be love

that I love you with.
When we get home,

there will be our kitchen, the dishes undone.
There will be our bedroom.

What is it you eventually recognized in my face
that allowed you to believe me?

Beauty that did not come from you—
remember how it did not come from you?

As white sage does not come from the moon
but is found by it and lit.

The Buddhists say
that the front of the paper

cannot exist without the back.
Because there is a there,

there is a here. Chaparral,
the density of growth,

and the tattered chaps
the mappers wore through it

because they had to,
to keep walking without

being hurt. It is okay if we hurt
one another.

Chaparral needs fire
(the pinecones cannot open

otherwise). Love needs lover,
whose last lover was flood.

Venison

The deer is still alive
in the roadside grass.
In an hour, we'll cut her open,
her left hip broken, the bone
in her dark body; now the white Camaro
shocked in the night and the boy

wet faced in the backseat,
his parents at a loss by the hood,
too young to have meant
any of it: the giving
or taking. They are glad for our headlights,
glad for our rifle.

Her head still on, she hangs
outside our kitchen window
for the blood to drip, skin
pulled down like a shirt.

I watch my husband undress her
with a knife. I wash the blue plates.
When I turn the water off, I can hear
his blade unmoor muscle, sail
through her fascia.

We put her leg and buttock
on the wooden table, where we
will gather her between us
to eat all year. It is all I see:
a thing, alive, slowly becoming my own body.

C-Section

This is the way we came
to remember the world.
We opened the woodstove

in October and found
the fire we'd laid in March,
but not lit, the day

we realized the day
itself would keep us warm.
An accidental kindness we paid ourselves:

forgetting the world and finding it
comprised, like kindling, of sunlight,
after thirty-one hours,

and your believing head wedged
where I was trying to open
again the prayer

I'd somehow painted shut,
storing my gratitude
instead on the earth,

which, from our hospital room,
we almost exited, you and I. Or entered.
It would have been difficult

to believe: the curvature of the earth,
but some did. Mostly mariners
who watched ships appear

portion by portion: mast
then hull, like a person
approaching from over a hill.

I believed
at least one of us
must know the way,

your helpless body unable
to escape my helpless body,
or appear

beyond the curve. Your bare
and tiny shoulders
would have stilled the waves.

Seed and Fugue

The carrot seeds dyed blue in the dirt,
the best butternut opened,
its white eyes unnumbered, unblinking,
twinning in the tilth. The garlic is so patient
when we keep it, sugar snap, its own held hand, small,
bulbous beet seed, angiosperm, cilantro and coriander,
your seed, which is half-human, never alone,
will grow in me, already
containing her own: the story begun inside
the story not started. Winged maple, marble of yolk
and albumen knows to make two voice boxes, one throat:
wood thrush who accompanies herself in song,
running cedar who runs, mayapple broadleaf
will shield her one ovary. The firefly's lit response,
crepuscular, planted on the ground.
I am the ground—you come down,
blinking. When heat is lifted
and dispersed by the light that's waited
all day under the grass,
I stay below mimicking
no star, the mountains
too slick for climbing, the moon
full to term and caught
without her skin.

Week Five: Measure

My husband carries a stone
in his pocket.

Each week he finds a bigger one.
I carry a child.

This week we carry twins
smooth as unripe dates.

He lifts his to see
how small

you still are.
I have nothing to hold

to be sure
you are breathing.

I used to keep
the moon for company,

the unmeasured sky
to keep me from want.

Now I keep this stone
growing between my hips

and breathe for it—my habit
your inheritance,

my breath measuring length for yours,
by which you'll measure everything

for a while, I who am still a child,
you already a grandmother and gone.

What is it you, conceived, are to do?
And your twin?

The stone will be a stone,
its own inheritance and time.

You will rise and grow full
on the air

in our blood. You will learn to breathe
how I breathe.

What else is there to do?

Week Twelve: Taproot

This time, when I talk to you,
I hold the girl

who lived inside my body.
She is fifteen, thirteen, eight.

To calm her, I trace her eyebrows
and shoulders. I follow the dark

strands of her hair. I peer into the furnace
to see how hurt is made.

She requires her body now.
She is still terrified.

It is not her body,
but her parents' bodies;

how beautiful their human forms,
how unremarkable

their insecurities. She is stunning.
I tell her this

and mean it, as I would mean it
if she were not me

but another, alive
and kind; her blemished

skin transparent now,
her hidden body, taking shape.

You are my daughter,
only conceived.

I feed you
with a store of love I've gathered

like a taproot
since my birth.

When I talk to you this time,
I hold the girl with that love.

I tell her the things
I will need her to know.

Relativity

Suspecting that large bodies bend space,
they only needed

to observe starlight bent by the sun and so
waited three years for a suitable eclipse

and led an expedition
to Crimea where they were taken

by the Russian army
and the beginning of World War I.

Einstein was sitting in a chair
in the patent office where he worked

when he had the thought:
If a person falls freely, he will not feel his own weight.

Later he called this the happiest thought in his life.
Though "happiest" here

may be better translated from the German
as "most fortunate."

When Einstein's son Eduard
asked him why he was famous, he responded that people

are like blind beetles who walk
the curved circumference of a branch,

not knowing the branch curves. He told Eduard
he could see the curve.

They were estranged by the time Eduard was old enough to send letters.
If a person fell freely,

the observer would not be able to tell
if he were subject to the force of gravity

or acceleration. He would not know
if he were falling, or floating in space.

Week Thirty-Eight: Mitosis

The moon will pull you out without shoes.
You are finishing your chores, forming

your hands and fingerprints.
I tell you, the stars are large

and low. I tell you
you must come see.

Put your work down, the cell has opened
and split. This is how

you have rendered inside me,
our solitude a two-way mirror.

In the snow that you won't remember,
the moon will give you her shoes.

I will call you born,
will tell you:

Once the rock of the moon
was part of the earth, broke off,

and the earth, overcome by levity,
spun faster, pulled

the moon so close it appeared
on the horizon enormous. See,

once there was no sky,
only proximity, only moon.

In the story
of our mitosis

the sky flies open,
the moon appears.

How can I hold you, child
when your body is mine, your middle, my own?

Nine times the moon has spooled. I've spun
a child in my belly, enormous—

and soon you will rest
like skin on my arm,

but not this close again.
I have never touched you.

I cannot see the moon,
the entire sky subsumed.

In Cleaning

the room where I want to rest,
I find my hands and am able

again to see you—
clear eyed where we left one another—

last year in the passenger's seat,
having woken after Colorado, which was beautiful

and which I did not wake you for,
wanting all the aspens,

all the golden, quaking aspens, and their silence
for myself.

Arrival

When the moon cast
a shadow for each tree
the same direction

on the snow,
it did not cross
or entangle them.

When you appeared
in the lambent world,
it was not on a long

or wooded walk anywhere,
not dropped or torn
from my waxing belly,

or directly
like royalty
at the bright trumpet

of the operating room,
my troubled form
gone gibbous.

It was before that,
when he and I
rubbed two cells together

because that was what we had.
No, before that too,
and never

was there a moment
when you were not
already

in the motion
of materials—of love,
which we call atoms

because we must
call it something—
turning to the sun,

the seed that is the fruit
that's already the seed begun
again, my body falling

into its middle.
Your shadow
casts itself now,

discrete from mine,
on the snow.
You've come

without arrival
and have made me human,
which is to say animal,

small mammal,
which is to say
that your face, the moon,

is tilted up now
of your own volition, reflecting,
producing, light.

II

River and Fugue

Narration, Transubstantiation

God is an infinite sphere, the center of which is everywhere,
the circumference nowhere.

1.

The peony, which was not open this morning, has opened,
falling over its edges

like the circumference of God, still clasped
at the center:

my two-month-old daughter's hand
in Palmar reflex, having endured

from the apes: ontogeny
recapitulating phylogeny, clutching for fur.

Her face is always tilted up when I carry her,
her eyes, always blue. She is asking

nothing of the sky, nothing
of the pileated woodpeckers,

their directionless wings, directed bodies,
the unmoved moving.

2.

Hold still,
song of the wood thrush,

smell of the creek
and the locust flowers, white as wafers

on the branches, communion: pistil, stamen, bee.
Hold still.

She doesn't say
a word.

3.

When we eat,
what we eat is the body

of the world.
Also when we do not eat.

She is asking the sky for milk.
Take and eat, we tell her,

this is my body
which is given for you

who are here now,
though you were not,

though you will be old
then absent again: sad

to us thinking forward in time
but not back. Not sad to you at all.

The peony whose circumference
is everywhere, you whose head

now is weighted to my chest,
the creek stringing its lights

along next to us,
the peony which has opened.

Night Weaning

My daughter speaks
two words in the night
and I am ladled from sleep
and have to turn the map
three times in my head

to find
my own position
in the bed,
the bed's position
in the room.

I cannot tell it is the room
I sleep in every night,
the windows open,
the air inhaled
to the house.

She is learning to chart
her wants. She says,
hi. She says,
milk. The open water
of the night-light

makes her breath
on my breast
a center
in the sea.
The floured moon

of her cheek
pulls the tide—
gravity a rope
between two
turning bodies—

it shines a bent course
from where we stand,
the fan on the ceiling, slow
and wheeling
the many muted stars.

She wakes
thirsty, and I
am an ocean
swelling to break
the shore.

To the Cardinal, Attacking His Reflection in the Window

It is your very self, I tell him.
He has never seen me.

His quick coin of breath disappears on the glass as it forms,
air that feeds his bones their portion

willingly as it feeds mine. He spends his here,
besieged by the dull birds who gather,

whom he cannot touch, his own feathers
red as wrought blood.

How many selves, dear bird,
must you vanquish?

In the mornings, his wings are backlit. They are beating,
cruciform, hollow feather, hollow bone.

In the blizzard his furor is the only color,
the only shape. He is waiting

for the coward to come out. There is nothing
all winter he has saved to eat.

I saw a female the day before he left.
Her beak just as orange, her body, calm, watched his.

I made voices for her: variations on the pride
and hemmed patience of women I'd known

whose husbands did insistent, strong,
and strange things. Maybe she knew it was spring. I didn't.

The next day he came once
to throw the bright dime of his life to the walled world,

as if to make sure it was not feather
against feather that hurt him.

River and Fugue

All afternoon
I have sat
in the middle
of the river,
disrupting the animals
who live in it and come
to resemble it:
river otter made
of its same
long muscle,
blue heron wings
taking after the sky.
And the deer
in dun grass.
How long
has she turned
her quiet head
to fix my sight?
Now she runs,
and here I still am.
Everything ascends
the wood thrush song.
Slant light climbs
from the piled hay;
my daughter is growing
this way:
most of time
is midafternoon,
this moment
becoming that
moment becoming this,
and she's changed
as a small cloud,
illuminated, cumulus,
completed as it moves.

Just so, she keeps
the company
of everything.
The fireflies blink.
They are weighted
by nothing, but want
gravity more
than they want
the moon,
which shines anyway
with borrowed light
that I take
as proof
of wealth
or delight.

Camera Obscura

My friend could feel the maples not being there,
even in the dark—the consent of weight

to gravity's long petition; all
the captured space of them, released.

The first trees had fallen in the first storm,
which she spent in a cancer ward in Maine.

In the clean purview of her heartache
the hospital had been an airport, thin walled,

everyone waiting to leave
when it's time, or past, for their departures.

She could feel the sap run
after them stepping from the gate into nothing.

In the snow, we'd collected it in a bucket
the size of my chest cavity and boiled it,

clear as water, until it obscured,
became apparent, sweetened all day in the tiny kitchen,

as if to say to the house, the maples:
don't you see what happens?

In the dark chamber of the heart
the image is reversed, upended,

projected on the wall, roots up,
branches taking the whole yard.

And light,
a guest I had not readied the room for,

did not see approaching,
the window covered by leaves.

Narrative

The interior of the car
has gone dark around her car seat,

the lighted highway is flat. I am telling
my daughter a story in which I am a deer

she comes across on the beach,
and with whom she travels

from the ocean to the mountains
and home in a single, hot day,

just to smell the hay ferns,
just to let the creek cool her.

Every moment of this is true
though nobody knows the next word.

And my daughter, nearly
a person, almost a story,

is full of comprehension.

III

And I You

For every atom belonging to me as good belongs to you.

—Walt Whitman

Week Ten: Plum

I.

My body, which has never died,
has two hearts again today,
and how many
inside the second?

This body, which has been planted
in ears and kidneys,
fingers and formed lungs, a person almost
the size of a plum, unbecome,

her own seed already in her.
This body, which is two bodies
and a thousand more in either
direction of time—the wake of the present—

has died ten thousand times, planted
as it is in the mud
where the plum must grow,
planted as it is in the dew.

II.

The moon may never have been a plum.
Look at her, having
dropped the dark robe of her skin;
you would not know it.

III.

I tell the collared dove: I am sown
—a body inside a body—for the rain to soak.
I carry her father, and his mother, and hers.

The field adores the seed, affords
the farmer, who frets, a task.
Every flower faces away.

I'm looking for what they watch.
The path through the field
leads to nothing but the field.

The dove calls three syllables:
all morning, compassion,
my daughter, all the night.

IV.

My own cells, planted by my father
and my mother who breathed
for me for some time,

the sun was their bodies
before it was mine,
was the bread and the fish

their parents ate, and the steel
and the ash. Who took
the bread and the fish?

I can't remember any of it.

If joy is watching a person bear
a pitcher of water across the field
where you are working,

if happiness is drinking it,
then I will watch the leaves, who watch
the sun go without flinching,

while my own heart opens and closes
the shutters
of my ribs every time.

The World Tips Back

Here is Hipparchus of Nicaea, looking at his globe,
turning art into technology, instrument into assumption.

He is not the first to name planets
after wanderers, or try to fix the stars.

Because he has no word for "arc," he sees circles
as completed: imagines whorled wool, whorled plants,

whorled planets, bound
only by themselves. Tonight my daughter said,

listen to my ear, and pulled my face to hers.
I want a word for distraction from one's child

by photos of one's child on one's phone. Bound up
with technologies of observation, would I hasten

dawn to the night? I would like
to fix the stars; the model and the one observing it

confused, which is to say, fused
together. While I fix on the chart, the stars move,

the arc long yet bending.
Perhaps it is not an arc at all

but a whorl. My theory of the universe
looks like the tools I have to measure it,

and somewhere I missed
what I did not know to see.

So we explained the eclipse, but not
the election, pointed from her height

to the altering light.
This morning, rain

had the house waking late.
She climbed into bed between us

saying, *The sun tips the world.*
Then the cloud comes, and the world tips back.

Week Twenty: Indulgences

The trout opens
and closes its mouth
to drown in the air,
a line in its jaw.

The cut butternut
stems still weep,
secrete what they offer
to their fruits, send everything

they have: *live,*
live, live. And my own father,
whom just this morning
I forgave for not driving away

from the parking lot
of the first-year dorm,
though I needed
my world to begin.

It was the last
moment he had
with the man he had
loved to be.

This morning in my car, parked
and pointed toward work,
the daughter I do not yet know
quickens inside me.

The daughter I do know, I can still feel
on my skin—her waking weight
from the morning's dark,
as real a centrifuge

on my shoulder
as my own accretion around it:
the beginning of a planet—
dust grains orbiting a pull.

Last night
her small clothes
hung on the line waiting,
and I loved them there
all night,
their drying
in the quiet.

The Death of My Mother's Father

I did not tell her that I wanted to see my uncles cry,
enough truth in saying I wanted to be there.

They didn't cry. Neither did they put anything
finally down: the weight of him,

clumsy in clean pine,
was wheeled instead over the frozen ground,
up the bothered hill,

while my uncles walked with free hands, bare shoulders,
then walked with his same sloped neck
to their cars.

The sun held to the skin tops of the sycamores
without our effort, held to our closed eyelids,

the weight of us, passed down to us,
never having been lifted, never set to the ground.

Yahrzeit

All I had for a menorah was a Coke bottle,
and the candle, crammed down its mouth
narrow end first to fit it,
would not light from the bottom end
though I'd excavated the wick, choked from the wax.
How else would I have loved
but by touching?

Yahrzeit, sunk fuzz ball of flame,
light to read Kaddish in transliteration. Oldest vowels
of mourners' mouths, pulled up on my phone:
a prayer that never mentions mourning
and never mentions death.

I wanted to miss him.
Instead there was a candle stuttering, and me
praising God's name in the dark,

and wax, whose job is not to spark
or hold a flame, but to keep the lit wick steady,
constant and disappearing.

Kaddish

. . . elevated and lauded be the name of the holy one, blessed far
beyond all the blessings and hymns, praises and consolations that
are spoken in the world; and say, Amen.

My father had grass in his pockets
at my cousin's bar mitzvah,
torn from the ground
near his father's grave. His own flesh,
formed from flesh, not symbol enough.

They didn't need to say the Kaddish
but they did, and removed nothing,
the polished wood of the pew still wearing overhead light,
the cloth folds of the men's tallit, the holy not needing
our sanctification, not needing even our silence.

Hashem

October came and the air lifted up,
unstuck itself from the roads,
from our backs.

They collected the corn
and I saw the land
for the first time, saw it

breathe without weight, rising
and falling, rising: skin
to skin with sunlight.

I watched a leaf disappear
eight thousand times on its fall,
leaving the air cooler, more bright.

And though I saw no good in its coming,
winter came, held out my own air
for me to see

that this whole time
I've been breathing,
laying months out flat

like cornhusks in the sun,
weaving with them small cups
to carry while I walk.

But the name,
like breath, finds gaps
that light can't,

and falls through
the spaces of my days,
my porous words.

So I cup my hands instead
to keep it; this gesture,
mistaken as an offering.

All I have is air,
and I've made none of it.
Held together by holding,

by not holding:
small lungs
that breathe by breathing.

IV

The More Extravagant Feast

Almanac

The garlic we pulled up when it went limp,
finally at the neck, was papered, fragile and whole,
cloves formed entire to themselves in the dark,

and I wanted to kiss the corner of your eye
where your skin folds from having folded there
with laughter; habit being also how thoughts crease.

But it was not time to think anything
and, for saying, I wanted all of the feeling that comes
in the slight predictability of speech,

as touch is better
when one has almost just expected where
and how it will come.

So I kissed you in a tent just as we both
were about to hope that I would.
What if touch is not speech,

but food? What food is this,
in the same place as our bodies?
The same field where we find

that whole potatoes have grown,
smooth-skinned meals out of dirt,
where the onion falls over at its nape and is ready.

Week Thirty-Four: Atomic

It was a heavy thing.
They hoisted it
in the desert for testing

but weren't sure
the wire would hold,
so stacked fifteen

old army mattresses
beneath it
should it drop.

They made it in a hurry
and kept no schematics.
Later they could

not replicate it.
One of the scientists,
when asked

how he'd built a particular tube,
described bending aluminum
around a Coke bottle.

There were pregnant women
of course in Virginia
and Nagasaki, who did not know

how to build what they built,
bending themselves
like rinds around the soft

seeds of their flesh, as though
they could keep
the world without,

without even a blueprint.
No idea of how it is done
even as it is done.

Helping

I cut a cantaloupe from its rind and hold it, scalped
and slipping. Inside it, there are seeds in folding rows,
dark in the concentric hollow, and I don't know how
I will remove them,

and I don't know how they keep one another,
in loose grasp, from falling,
or what they would touch if they fell.

Standing on a chair to help, she notices and is startled
by the dent at the base of her thumb that appears
when she splays her hand in the seeds.

Morning in the kitchen, light bright metal in the sink,
I go to stand beside her,
show her my own matching hollow.

Slowly I am removing from my belief
those who, I was taught, understand things,
the calm ones in clean shoes.

Tenderly I am removing them
from the walls, like fire escapes that have allowed me
to sit inside without concern.

Inside I find that we are standing, together at the sink,
and we begin to cut the melon
whichever way we can.

Furniture

She looked at me without seeing that I could see her.
I was a new thing in her house,
in the mornings sitting across the table,
braless in the sunlight that came
rectangular through the doorframe
where the young cats curled.
Reminded, she lifted her own small, heavy breasts
one at a time, trying vacantly to look at them.

At night she watched TV. I sat with her,
her left side fallen, her speech repeating
and without consonants.
That cowboy keeps kissing all the women,
I said of the telenovela,
because I could think of how to say it in Spanish,
and because he did. She laughed
and looked away from it to me,
the black-and-white TV light
all over the furniture, flickering,
taking the walls on and off the room.

Waking Up the Bell

The poem is the slag heap,
and what I keep I keep.

The axe I did not make, the trees
do what I can't: converting light

for when it's gone. The fire
and the forges

call the metals back
like meteorites from orbit.

The ore is that this changes me,
extracts me from myself.

The iron tonsil of the bell
I neither wrought nor swung

cleaves hours into halves,
muscles to my bone.

It scores my weeks,
spills them

one at a time
in the lap of the ferrous valley.

We'll break them open this way,
melt them back to days.

Carrot

Take all summer,
your ember

from the sun,
its walking meditation.

Store it in small
vaults of light

to keep
the rest of us

when winter seals
around each day.

We'll flicker
to the table.

We'll gather
to your orange flame.

Table

It is unset,
my heart:

small framed,
smoothed stone;

yours a bare room,
its windows thrown,

and the table
in the middle.

Beneath its foot
on the tile floor, have been

positioned rocks,
which have taken years to find

and angle into place.
Here is one

dislodged for you.
Here, the uneven leg,

here the meal.

Engagement

When I picture you I will picture you
eating small plums off the ground by the fistful.

I am walking far from the plum tree
I showed you

in the corner
of the weedy orchard.

I have been throwing away the possibility
that I will be married to you

(I am engaged to be married to you).
I am throwing it away again

and when it lunges back,
away again,

because I believe I can mow a meadow
between me and my need, my need

and your fear.
My mother once traced

a story on my face
while I lay on the floor.

We didn't know the story's name.
Her finger illustrated the hero's long hair

over my eyebrow, her voyage
down the swell of my cheek

to talk with my mouth
through the blue thick of sleep,

then upstairs, alone,
to her high bedroom

on my chin, with the window
and the moon.

A vow is a thing I want to know I can do
I told the dumb phone.

It helps, sometimes,
to narrate.

The old man with the stiff hip
and blue shorts walks up the steep street

two yards from his wife.
She is carrying the groceries.

It is impossible to tell
which of them is doing

the insisting: how necessary every
thing is.

The More Extravagant Feast

The buck is thawing a halo on the frosted ground,
shot in our field predawn.

Last night we pulled a float in the Christmas parade.
It was lit by a thousand tiny lights.

My daughter rode in my lap and was thrilled
when the float followed us. Ours is a small town.

Everyone was there. And their faces,
not seeing ours, fixed behind us, were an open sea,

a compound sea of seas that parted
under our gaze. And Santa was bright,

though my daughter shied from the noise of him.
She studied the red and white fur of his suit.

She woke this morning when the rifle fired outside.
I lifted her to see the sunrise

and her father, kneeling above the buck's body
in the middle distance. She asked if they would be cold.

I brought him gloves and warm water, knelt with him
in the spare light by the buck, who steamed, whose liver

and heart, kept so long dark,
spilled onto the winter grass,

whose open eyes saw none of it, realized
nothing of my husband's knife

slicing open his abdomen, his rectum. The puncture
of his diaphragm startled me more than the gunshot,

opening a cavern of blood that poured
over his white belly. I did not

understand the offering, but loved it,
the fur red, white, incoherent. Somehow cleaner.

When I come back in, she asks me to draw a picture
of her father on the hill. I pick her up—the miracle

of her lungs that grew inside me,
kept long dark—her working heart

let out into the rounder world,
the more extravagant feast. The miracle

of her dad on the hill as we draw him
in his big coat, warm. Afterward,

how he and I hold each other
differently, feeling

the collections of muscles
and organs held

somehow together. The miracle
of bodies, formed whole like fruits,

skins unruptured and
containing the world.

Notes

The lines "that the front of the paper / cannot exist without the back" in "Field Guide to the Chaparral" and the image of carrying a pitcher in "Week Ten: Plum" come from Dharma talks given by Thich Nhat Hanh at Plum Village in 2014.

"Relativity" owes a debt to Walter Isaacson for his biography *Einstein: His Life and Universe.*

The epigraph to "Narration, Transubstantiation" is of debated authorship, and originates in *The Book of the Twenty-Four Philosophers*, thought to have been composed between the fourth and twelfth centuries.

"The World Tips Back" is after Colin Webster's talk on classical astronomy, "Time, Technology, and the History of Ancient Science," delivered on April 27, 2017, at Washington and Lee University.

The epigraph to "Kaddish" is from a version of the Mourner's Kaddish, as interpreted by the poet.

"Week Thirty-Four: Atomic" uses information from Eric Schlosser's book *Command and Control: Nuclear Weapons, the Damascus Accident, and the Illusion of Safety.*

Acknowledgments

My gratitude for the generous support of the Academy of American Poets, the Lenfest Grant, the Katharine Bakeless Nason Scholarship, the UCI Humanities Center International Travel Grant, and the English and Environmental Studies departments at Washington and Lee University, and to the editors, staff, and readers of the following publications in which these poems first appeared:

Ecotone: "Venison" and "*Camera Obscura*," originally published as "Once Home,"

Pleiades: "Narration, Transubstantiation" and "To the Cardinal, Attacking His Reflection in the Window"

The Southern Review: "Field Guide to the Chaparral"

The Squaw Valley Review: "Helping," originally published as "Becoming Sisters"

Tin House: "The More Extravagant Feast"

Wellspring: Poetry for the Journey: "Narrative"

"Venison," "In Cleaning," and "Helping" were collected by the Academy of American Poets

A selection of these poems appear in the chapbook *The Ones We Have*

• • •

I am grateful to the people who have cared about these poems, among them: Chantz Erolin and Jeff Shotts for their capacious, kind minds; what a great joy that anyone would be so present with me in the work. Thank you to the whole Graywolf team. To Sally Mann whose generosity I cannot fathom, Elise Sheffield with whom I could walk forever, Justin Rigamonti for seeing me as well as these poems fully, what a gift to be so known. To Anna Lena Phillips Bell, Sierra Bellows, Michelle Burke, John Casteen, Brandon Courtney, Camille Dungy, Ross Gay,

Mark Jarman, Ilya Kaminsky, Veronica Kuhn, Lulu Miller, Rabia Sandage, Elizabeth Sauder, Allison Seay, Bruce Smith, Beth Staples, Taylor Walle, Lesley Wheeler, and the Monastics of Plum Village—thank you all for your conversation.

To my parents who have said, before I or they read: "stop this day and night with me and you shall possess the origin of all poems." To my brother. Thank you for celebrating.

To Walt Whitman.

To Li-Young Lee and the rooms of light his work opens for me. For the space to open into them, the honor is unspeakable.

And to Ben Eland who has been intimately invested in every one of these poems, their inspirations, images, commas; who is the most thoughtful, capable father and partner a person could ask for; who brings my thoughts, as my days, closer to themselves.

Leah Naomi Green is the author of *The More Extravagant Feast*, winner of the Walt Whitman Award of the Academy of American Poets, and *The Ones We Have*, winner of the Flying Trout Press Chapbook Prize. She teaches English and environmental studies at Washington and Lee University. Green and her family homestead and grow food in the mountains of Virginia.

The text of *The More Extravagant Feast* is set in Whitman.
Book design by Rachel Holscher.
Composition by Bookmobile Design and Digital Publisher
Services, Minneapolis, Minnesota.
Manufactured by Sheridan on acid-free, 30 percent
postconsumer wastepaper.